a CHANGE of HEART

Story by **Alice Walsh**

Art by **Erin Bennett Banks**

NIMBUS
PUBLISHING

Nimbus Publishing Limited
3731 Mackintosh St, Halifax, NS, B3K 5A5
(902) 455-4286 nimbus.ca

Printed and bound in China

NB1175

Cover illustration: Erin Bennett Banks
Cover design: Heather Bryan
Interior design: Jenn Embree

Library and Archives Canada Cataloguing in Publication

Walsh, Alice (E. Alice), author
A change of heart / story by Alice Walsh ; art by Erin Bennett Banks.
    Issued in print and electronic formats.
    ISBN 978-1-77108-371-3 (bound).—ISBN 978-1-77108-372-0 (pdf)

1. Phillips, Lanier, 1923-2012—Juvenile literature. 2. African American civil rights workers—Biography—Juvenile literature. 3. St. Lawrence (N.L.)—Biography—Juvenile literature. 4. Truxtun (Ship)—Juvenile literature. 5. Shipwrecks—Newfoundland and Labrador—Juvenile literature. I. Banks, Erin Bennett, 1978-, illustrator II. Title.

E185.97.P45W34 2016   j305.896'073   C2015-908183-1
                                                    C2015-908184-X

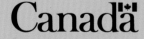 

Nimbus Publishing acknowledges the financial support for its publishing activities from the Government of Canada through the Canada Book Fund (CBF) and the Canada Council for the Arts, and from the Province of Nova Scotia. We are pleased to work in partnership with the Province of Nova Scotia to develop and promote our creative industries for the benefit of all Nova Scotians.

For Lanier's children: Terry Phillips, Vonzia Phillips, Norton Phillips,
Caulda Pope, Valerie Miller, and Louwane Almeida.
–AW

To my grandparents, with much love.
–EBB

Lithonia, Georgia, 1930

Lanier sat up in the darkness trembling with fear.

He could hear his parents' whispered voices in the kitchen. He pictured them sitting by the window with the lights out. Earlier in the evening a neighbour had come with a warning: "The Klan's gonna be riding tonight." Such a warning struck fear in the hearts of children and adults alike.

Lanier pulled his knees to his chest. Nothing terrified him more than the Ku Klux Klan in their white robes. Their hooded eyes glared through the holes in the pillowcases they wore over their faces. He'd seen the Klan drag men from their homes and beat them in front of their family. They burned down houses, barns, and schools.

Please, he prayed silently, *don't let them stop here tonight.*

Years passed, but things did not get easier for Lanier and his family. Because of a law called Jim Crow, Black people could not eat in the same restaurants or even drink from the same water fountains as white people. Black children could not attend school with white children. On top of all that, the Klan continued to terrorize Black families.

Why do they hate us? Lanier asked himself. But he knew the answer. The Klan hated them because their skin was black.

Resentment grew inside Lanier like a wound that would not heal.

In 1941, the year Lanier turned eighteen, the United States joined the Second World War. Seeing a chance to escape the racism in Georgia, he joined the navy. However, attitudes did not get any better. Aboard Lanier's ship, the USS *Truxton*, Black sailors had separate sleeping quarters from the white sailors. Lanier and his fellow Black sailors were also expected to serve as mess attendants, laundering clothes, shining shoes, and washing dishes. They were not allowed to eat in the dining room and instead took their meals in a small pantry. They often ate standing up because there were no chairs.

One cold February night while sailing to Newfoundland, the *Truxtun* ran into a storm. The ship tossed and pitched as it steamed through the choppy sea.

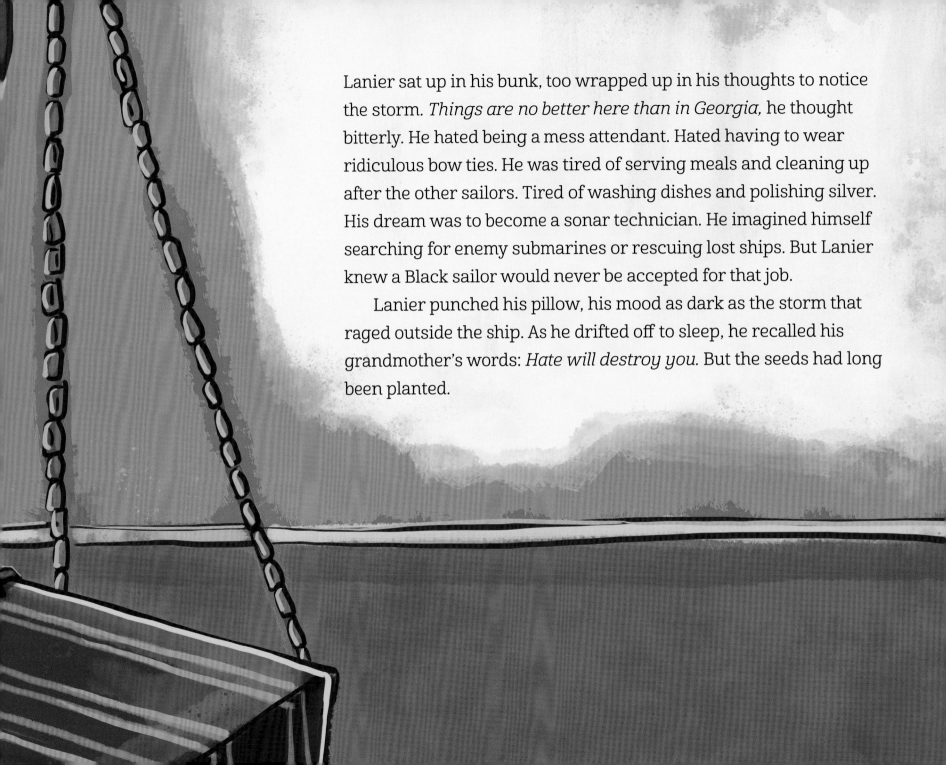

Lanier sat up in his bunk, too wrapped up in his thoughts to notice the storm. *Things are no better here than in Georgia,* he thought bitterly. He hated being a mess attendant. Hated having to wear ridiculous bow ties. He was tired of serving meals and cleaning up after the other sailors. Tired of washing dishes and polishing silver. His dream was to become a sonar technician. He imagined himself searching for enemy submarines or rescuing lost ships. But Lanier knew a Black sailor would never be accepted for that job.

Lanier punched his pillow, his mood as dark as the storm that raged outside the ship. As he drifted off to sleep, he recalled his grandmother's words: *Hate will destroy you.* But the seeds had long been planted.

Without warning, Lanier was jolted awake by the grinding of steel against rock. The impact hurled him from his bunk onto the floor. "What's going on?" he shouted, scrambling in the darkness for his shoes.

Panicked sailors rushed to the *Truxtun*'s deck, a fierce wind driving sleet into their faces.

Where are we? Lanier wondered as a searchlight swept over a bleak landscape. Steep, jagged cliffs rose hundreds of feet above him. Everything was covered in ice and snow.

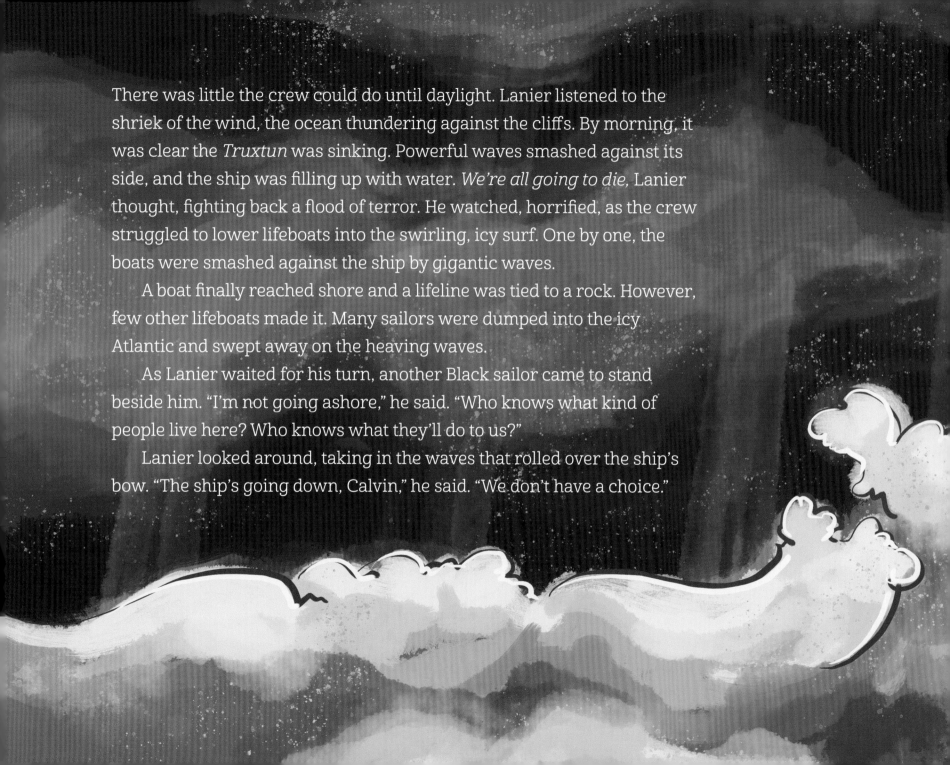

There was little the crew could do until daylight. Lanier listened to the shriek of the wind, the ocean thundering against the cliffs. By morning, it was clear the *Truxtun* was sinking. Powerful waves smashed against its side, and the ship was filling up with water. *We're all going to die,* Lanier thought, fighting back a flood of terror. He watched, horrified, as the crew struggled to lower lifeboats into the swirling, icy surf. One by one, the boats were smashed against the ship by gigantic waves.

A boat finally reached shore and a lifeline was tied to a rock. However, few other lifeboats made it. Many sailors were dumped into the icy Atlantic and swept away on the heaving waves.

As Lanier waited for his turn, another Black sailor came to stand beside him. "I'm not going ashore," he said. "Who knows what kind of people live here? Who knows what they'll do to us?"

Lanier looked around, taking in the waves that rolled over the ship's bow. "The ship's going down, Calvin," he said. "We don't have a choice."

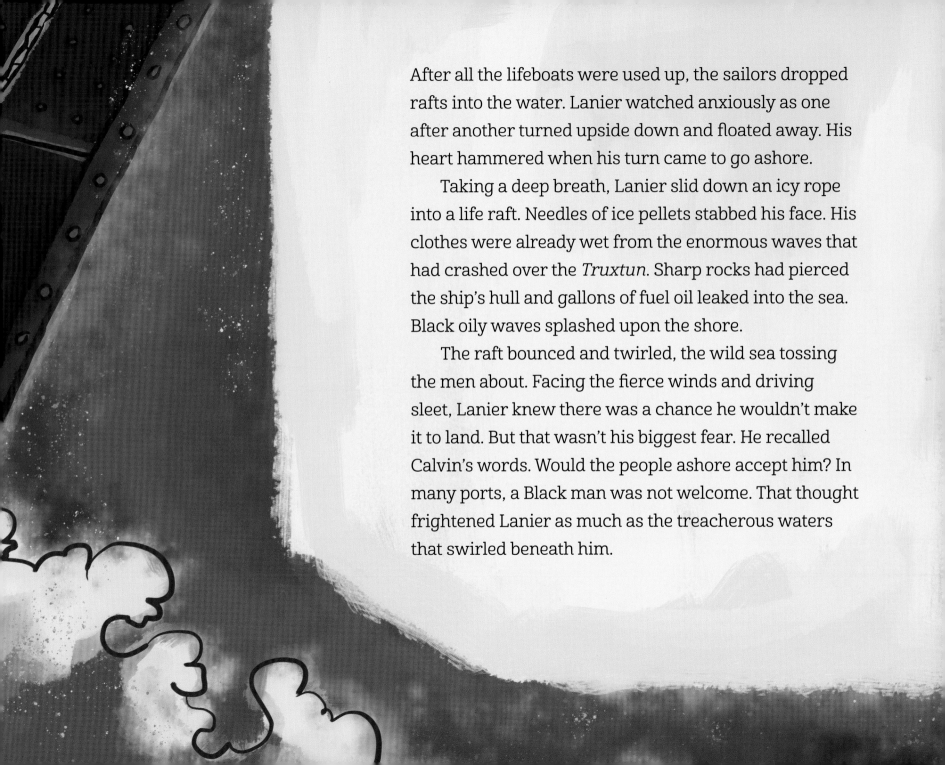

After all the lifeboats were used up, the sailors dropped rafts into the water. Lanier watched anxiously as one after another turned upside down and floated away. His heart hammered when his turn came to go ashore.

Taking a deep breath, Lanier slid down an icy rope into a life raft. Needles of ice pellets stabbed his face. His clothes were already wet from the enormous waves that had crashed over the *Truxtun*. Sharp rocks had pierced the ship's hull and gallons of fuel oil leaked into the sea. Black oily waves splashed upon the shore.

The raft bounced and twirled, the wild sea tossing the men about. Facing the fierce winds and driving sleet, Lanier knew there was a chance he wouldn't make it to land. But that wasn't his biggest fear. He recalled Calvin's words. Would the people ashore accept him? In many ports, a Black man was not welcome. That thought frightened Lanier as much as the treacherous waters that swirled beneath him.

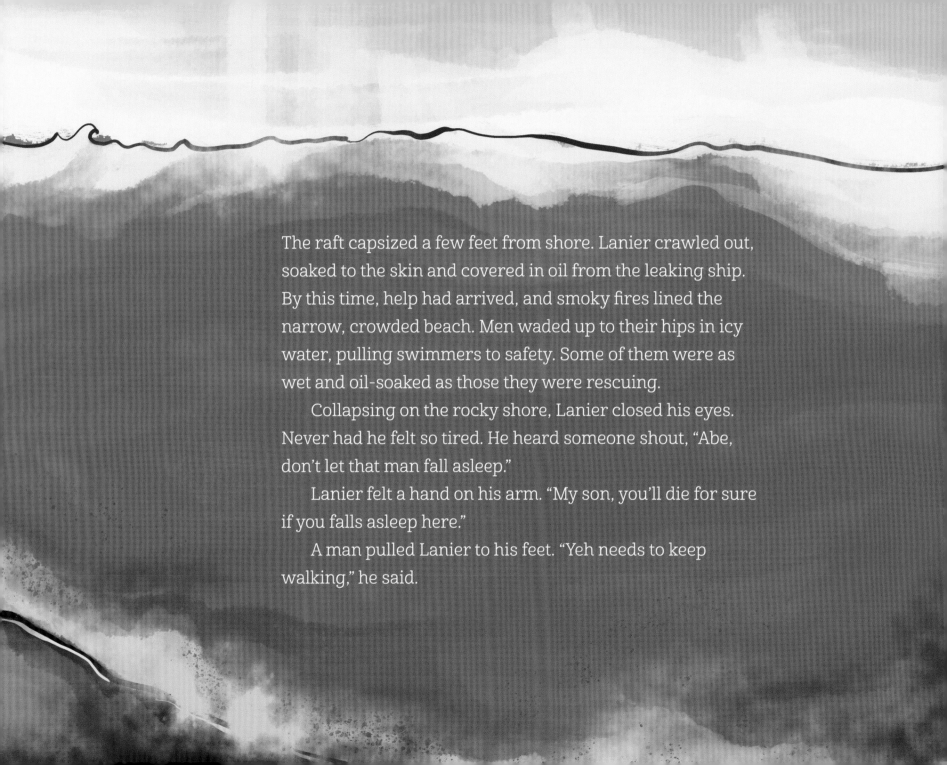

The raft capsized a few feet from shore. Lanier crawled out, soaked to the skin and covered in oil from the leaking ship. By this time, help had arrived, and smoky fires lined the narrow, crowded beach. Men waded up to their hips in icy water, pulling swimmers to safety. Some of them were as wet and oil-soaked as those they were rescuing.

Collapsing on the rocky shore, Lanier closed his eyes. Never had he felt so tired. He heard someone shout, "Abe, don't let that man fall asleep."

Lanier felt a hand on his arm. "My son, you'll die for sure if you falls asleep here."

A man pulled Lanier to his feet. "Yeh needs to keep walking," he said.

Lanier felt numb from the cold, but he mustered enough strength to keep moving.

The man named Abe looked across the harbour. "Terrible, my son, terrible," he said, shaking his head.

Lanier followed his gaze to where the doomed *Truxtun* lay on its side. Dozens of men clung to the safety lines on the ship's port side. Great swells rolled over the ship, taking most of the men with it. In the harbour, men desperately clung to rafts and wreckage. Lanier's heart broke thinking of his Black comrades who chose to stay on the ship rather than face the racism they believed awaited them ashore.

"Where am I?" Lanier asked.

"A couple miles from the town of St. Lawrence on the southeast coast of Newfoundland," said Abe.

"Canada?"

"No, my son, we got nothin' to do with Canada."

Abe walked Lanier to the base of the cliff. They watched as ropes were dropped down the side to pull sailors to the top. Men lowered themselves down the cliffs to carry up those too weak or exhausted to hold on.

Lanier stumbled, feeling a wave of exhaustion.

"We'll get yeh to the mine house soon," Abe promised. "Get yeh all fixed up, sure."

Lanier nodded gratefully, struggling to keep his eyes open.

Lanier opened his eyes and looked around a dimly lit room. He was lying on a table covered by a sheet and couldn't stop shivering. *Where am I?* he wondered. He was aware of voices—women's voices, soft and soothing. The smell of oil was so strong he almost gagged. Men around him were coughing and retching.

Bits of memory drifted in and out of Lanier's mind. *Going up a steep cliff...wrapped in a blanket on a horse-drawn sleigh...being carried into a building.* Were the memories real, or had he dreamed them?

Lanier became aware of two white women standing over him. One was scrubbing his arm with a washcloth. He closed his eyes. Drifting in and out of sleep, he listened to snatches of their conversation.

"Never seen hair that curly, Violet. Sure, me own hair don't curl that good even after I perms it."

Violet rubbed briskly at Lanier's skin. "Poor soul, the oil's gone right into his pores. Can't get it off no matter how hard I scrubs!"

Lanier felt a stab of fear: The women had never seen a Black man before. How would they react when they learned the truth? Would he be turned out in the ice and snow? In Georgia a Black man would be run out of town for talking with a white woman. He could hear his grandmother's voice in his head: *Never bother a white woman. Always remember, a white woman best have the sidewalk to herself.*

"It won't come off, ma'am," Lanier said shyly. "It's the colour of my skin."

"Never seen skin that dark," Violet said, but she sounded relieved.

At that moment a man came by. "We'll be loading the flatbed soon, sir," he said.

Lanier stared at him. No white man had ever called him sir.

"He's ready to go, Bill," said Violet. "Take him to my house."

Lanier was too stunned to speak. Had he heard right? Was this woman offering to take him into her home?

Violet pointed to a pile of clothing on a nearby table. "Make sure you dresses warm," she told Lanier.

Lanier blinked back tears. Until now, all his experiences with white people had been marked by hatred and violence. In that single moment, he felt all his fear, bitterness, and anger melt away. It was as if a great burden had been lifted from his heart, setting him free.

During his stay, Violet cared for Lanier as if he were her own son. He was given a warm bed. Violet fed him hot soup. The family included him in their conversations. For the first time in his life, Lanier felt worthy as a human being.

Lanier's health recovered, but more importantly, he no longer carried bitterness and resentment. He knew his life had been changed forever.

With a light heart, he walked to the truck that would drive him to the dock. A naval ship was waiting to take him home.

"Looks like the worst of the storm has passed," the driver said as Lanier climbed aboard.

Lanier gazed at the sky. The clouds were still dark, but the sun was trying to break through. "Yes," he agreed, "everything's going to be okay." The truck lurched forward and started down a long, bumpy road.

About Lanier Phillips

In 1957 Lanier Phillips became the first African American to graduate from the US Navy's sonar school. Throughout his career he won many awards, including the prestigious Lone Sailor Award. This award is presented to Sea Service Veterans who have distinguished themselves by drawing upon their experience to become successful in their later careers and lives. Other recipients of the award include President John F. Kennedy, President Gerald Ford, and US Secretary of State John Kerry.

Lanier also became active in the Civil Rights Movement. In March 1965, he joined Dr. Martin Luther King in the famous march from Selma to Montgomery, Alabama, to support civil rights for African Americans.

Lanier credits the people of St. Lawrence, Newfoundland, for his achievements. "They gave me the courage to fight for what was important," he said. He often called his experience in Newfoundland "A lesson in humanity and love for mankind." Every chance he got, he told stories of his shipwreck and the kind strangers who took him in, changing his life forever. "I was wounded in mind and soul," he said. "But I was healed in St. Lawrence, Newfoundland."

In 2008 Lanier received an honorary Doctor of Laws degree from Memorial University of Newfoundland. The award was presented to Lanier for what the university called his "resistance to and capacity to rise above repression." Three years later he was made an honorary member of the Order of Newfoundland and Labrador, the highest award in the province. In February 2012, the seventieth anniversary of the *Truxton* disaster, he travelled to Newfoundland to honour the 203 men who had perished. The only Black survivor of the shipwreck, Lanier Phillips died only months after his visit, at the age of eighty-eight.